MACRAME FOR ABSOLUTE BEGINNERS
in 2022

Best Pattern Book With Step-by-Step Pictures. Relax at Home and see How Easy it is to Create Low Budget Projects Like PLANT HANGERS, JEWELRY, WALL HANGINGS, BRACELET + WOW BONUSES

MW00904448

© Copyright 2021 - All rights reserved.

This document is geared towards providing exact and reliable information in regard to the topic and issue covered.

- From a Declaration of Principles which was accepted and approved equally by a Committee of the American Bar Association and a Committee of Publishers and Associations.

In no way is it legal to reproduce, duplicate, or transmit any part of this document in either electronic means or in printed format. All rights reserved.

The information provided herein is stated to be truthful and consistent, in that any liability, in terms of inattention or otherwise, by any usage or abuse of any policies, processes, or directions contained within is the solitary and utter responsibility of the recipient reader. Under no circumstances will any legal responsibility or blame be held against the publisher for any reparation, damages, or monetary loss due to the information herein, either directly or indirectly.

Respective authors own all copyrights not held by the publisher.

The information herein is offered for informational purposes solely and is universal as so. The presentation of the information is without contract or any type of guarantee assurance.

The trademarks that are used are without any consent, and the publication of the trademark is without permission or backing by the trademark owner. All trademarks and brands within this book are for clarifying purposes only and are owned by the owners themselves, not affiliated with this document.

Table of Contents

3

Introduction

Macramé is a decorative knot found in almost every culture, but it takes on different forms in different societies. Knot-tying is mainly performed by youth scouts and cadets, particularly in second-cycle institutions as part of their training sessions.

After its formal introduction as a topic in various universities, macramé art has grown in popularity. It's now used with other materials to create a wide range of beautiful works of art. Macramé is closely correlated with fashionable teenagers due to its fast development, great adaptability, and wide applications. This is a common fashion decoration that emerged in Eastern textiles and became a key component in developing each decorative garment, especially at the tent, and towel fringes.

Macramé is an Italian term used in Genoa. It became the most popular textile technique in conventional ways. Knots are used for several mnemonics, utilitarian, and superstitious purposes over time, and knotting emerged in early Egyptian culture in Africa, where knots were used in fishnet and decorative fringes. The Quipu, made of mnemonic knots (overhand knots), was used by the Incas of Peru to record and convey knowledge.

The use of knots, their shape, the color of a rope, and the knot itself all contributed to the complex meanings being conveyed. Knots were used in medicine (as slings for broken bones) and sports in ancient Greece, such as the Gordian knot, which was one such mystery. Both, early Egyptians and Greeks used the "Hercules knot" (square knot) on clothing, jewels, and pottery with magical or religious connotations.

While macramé art has been created and used for further development in most cultures to achieve both functional and artistic appeal, the final products differ depending on the culture. The ornamental usage of knotting separates ancient cultures and reflects intellectual growth. It is an art for people of all ages and skills. Today, macramé is commemorating the twentieth-century revival. Men and women work with their hands to produce utilitarian and aesthetic objects. Despite its importance, macramé is regarded as merely a shape knotting technique due to its simplicity and versatility. Although its value, macramé as a knotting technique is limited by its simplicity and current usability. Macramé is a vibrant, adaptable, and exploratory material that lends itself to processing and handling in product production and manufacturing in various ways. This has been a highly prized talent all over the world since its conception.

In the 13th century, the invention of macramé passed through Arabia. Spain spread it to the rest of Europe after the Moorish invasion of Turkey in the early 14th century, arriving in Italy and France in the early 14th and 15th centuries, and was later adopted into England in the late 17th century and mid-to-late 19th century during the Victorian era.

Historians and sailors are said to have disseminated this form of art around the world. Macramé had entered its dormant phase in China and America by the 1920s when it was used to make objects such as flower hangers, expertly made belts, and industrial containers.

Macramé has also been a perfect herbal therapy for people seeking detox procedures, and it aims to boost memories once again, making it a wonderful experience for everyone. Rope play and tying protects the hands and limbs while loosening the wrist and finger joints.

It will help calm the mind and spirit because it needs concentration, and the repetitive patterns will place a weaver in a meditative state. Also, stress is believed to be released by the fingertips, making macramé knotting a pleasurable experience. Macramé has the added benefit of enjoying the self-expression process by creating the intrinsic target concealed within.

16

Chapter 1: History, Meaning, and Purpose of Macramé

Macramé is a kind of ornamental work that consists of knotting and weaving coarse thread into a design. Some controversies suggest that the term macramé emerged from French roots, but most scholars believe it originated from the terms migramah and migrama, both words synonymous with spinning and head coverings in Arabic. The first documented "Macrameers" were Arabic weavers of the 13th century who began making decorative knots to protect the loose ends of the woven textiles, such as shawls and towels.

When most people imagine macramé, they imagine the results of the upsurge in the popularity of the textile technique during the 1970s—or hanging the plant, glass tabletops, multiple lampshades, pockets, and belts, and other bohemian-favored accessories. Although macramé blends in with many age patterns, its roots stretch back hundreds of years across oceans. Macramé has an amazing past. Let's start our journey into macramé's rich history.

Use of Netted Pots for Beauty and Practicality in Egypt

Rope-making in Egypt was extremely developed and well-known in Ancient Egypt.

It all started with a knot.

A knot is a basic process of bringing 2 loose ends together and connecting them. We never pay a second thought to the procedure, but there is so much more to a knot. Since the earliest humans, knots have been a regular companion of humankind who used them in practical application and often made it into mystical, scientific, theological, medical, creative, and decorative items. Macramé is one case where the basic act of knot-tying was turned into an art form by man.

The fragility of textile artifacts is a daunting challenge that archaeologist face—they disintegrate well before we can reveal them to examine and document. It was the same issue with the identification of the macramé origins. Experts confidently believe that knotting has been with humankind because man's need for building and work grew. The oldest visible instances of finding knots were dated between 15,000 and 17,000 BC. They estimate, though, the knotting could be 250,000 years old or even existed 2,500,000 years ago.

Origin and Distribution of Modern Macramé in the Middle East During 13th Century

In addition, the Crusaders, who conquered the Middle East between 1095–1228, also came into contact with the art. It is presumed that their spouses and maids, who were traveling with them, had learned this skill from the locals.

While today we consider macramé decorative art, its roots have been more utilitarian than decorative. This simplistic form of square knotting, aka macramé, was used by Arab weavers to secure the loose ends of their woven objects.

Macramé is mostly preferred by women nowadays, like other fiber crafts, but few of the very prominent and successful macrameers were no other than men—sailors, precisely. Understanding the versatility of the simple reef knot (or also known as a square knot) and the power of various hook knots to tie sails and fill cargo with the ropes, the early maritime explorers found that tying the knots could also relieve their boredom. Such sailors also started tying for months at sea, incorporating increasingly intricate knots into elegant designs for periodic functional applications, such as rope ladders and bell pulls. As the ships docked at different ports, the sailors often would sell or barter their products, and macramé's art—and popularization of nautical products such as twine and rope—started to spread to many nations, including China.

The Queen Obsessed by Lace (17th Century, Netherlands, and Great Britain)

Mary II was first exposed to macramé in the Netherlands (30 April 1662–28 December 1694) due to her marriage to William of Orange. Both king and queen shared a penchant for lace. Not only did she continue to adorn her clothing with lace, but she also created various styles of lace, including macramé, and taught her ladies the art of macramé in waiting. The British court recognizes her for bringing macramé to the ladies, where it became a mainstream craft.

Queen Charlotte was another Royal lady who cherished macramé. She was in charge of decorating the royal residence, and her macramé lace designs were trimmed into many of the furnishings. She built the trend in Georgian England for Macramé, which eventually became a popular past-time.

Ireland's Gift to American Macramé History in 1864

The most well-known silk thread manufacturers, Barbour from Ireland, arrived in Paterson, New Jersey, in 1864. This made the thread most widely used for macramé readily available to the US market.

Slumber Years and the Macramé Revival

There came a time when the macramé of the Victorian period vanished for over 80 years from traditional crafting techniques. During a 1940's publication, there are small references to the art, so it is safe to believe that the rationings and shortages of the world wars may have influenced this art much as they had on another similar embroidery. This, therefore, did not require the more realistic applications of knitting or stitching for some kind of decorative art. Females also joined the service when the people were fighting in the world wars.

The counterculture of the 1960s resurrected macramé and other artisan crafts, such as leatherwork, copper work, sewing, etc., as they rebelled against industrial manufacturing and mechanization.

The Macramé Golden Years in Victorian England

During the Victorian era, macramé excellence was said to be equal and even overshadowed what it was during the Hippie movement. Lace and lace-making were a major trend throughout the 19th century, particularly in the latter half. The fabrics of preference for the Victorian ladies were silk cord, while for delicate soft hands, the coarse rope used by sailors was considered rougher. Also, as it was already popular to create home trimmings, macramé was seen as a quicker and cheaper way to create trimmings for household items.

Cultural and Economic Influence on Macramé Evolution

It was Macramé, which reached its height in Victorian England. Macramé had already been a widely popular female hobby. As part of their schooling, many young ladies started learning macramé to become a lady. Home newspapers and magazines gave tips from table linens of macramé to the designing of curtains with macramé. Almost every fashionable house had some form of macramé, which adorned its interior.

The success of macramé diminished in the early 1900s, and although it didn't entirely vanish, the art was even more elusive in both practice and merchandise for a half-century. As a result, during the 1970s, people were suddenly going nuts again for the knots.

There have been devoted artists since the 70s who have introduced macramé from a domestic craft into galleries of artists all over the world. And today is no different. Some credit the return of macramé with the return of the houseplant trend, as a hanging garden takes up less space in smaller apartments. This can also explain why ball plants had become a hit in Japanese art. Yet, these were more costly and difficult to produce, and not ideal for all plants. So, a plant hanger was considered a good alternative. Macramé was part of the big artisan renaissance during the '60s. One explanation that seems valid is with the consciousness of the millennial generation about leading a greener lifestyle and a willingness to move closer to nature, but this is difficult for those in tiny apartments without a backyard. Hence, the next best option is hanging gardens. It may also explain why this phenomenon has become the Japanese style of kokedamas.

The fascinating aspect is how many countries and their citizens use macramé and other experts in the trade to generate income in impoverished places. Macramé art has now been embraced as one of the most significant methods for making apparel accessories in Ghana. This art form now provides an alternative method, especially for bag and shoe manufacturing, in the fashion industry. In the last few years, the number of younger consumers of macramé goods has witnessed tremendous growth. Today's youth is trendy, with a major focus on innovative, creative designs. Today, macramé art is a career for the youth and a symbol of the innovative growth of the young generation.

At the beginning of the feminist movement, macramé's comeback portrayed a wider cultural dichotomy—on the one hand, most of the women buckled expectations of traditional genders, such as marriage and then motherhood, to empower autonomy and sexual freedom and also financial freedom. On the other side, in their free time, they revived a craft that peaked in the era, remembered for its strict norms and conservative approach. Only they had a wild, grandiose, and uninhibited approach to the craft. In the 1970s, almost everything was made from macramé.

The era's largest macramé trend was a complete cry. The macramé owl's history is also a very omnipresent and ridiculous portrayal of craft, which is quite mysterious. Owls were one of the famous themes in home decor during the 1970s, and the trend might be associated with the United States, during 1971, because of the announcement made by the Forest Service to appoint Woodsy Owl as their logo. The character wore a red-feathered Robin Hood-esque green cap and asked people to "don't pollute but give a hoot!" Also, the owls are considered heavenly creatures in several cultures, which symbolize wisdom and bring good luck. Owls are among the most powerful and important animals in Feng Shui, and the Chinese practice from ancient times claims to use the energy which forces to create harmony between humans and their environment.

Macramé all but vanished during the 1980s, 1990s, and '00s as a home decor phenomenon, but the design has made a gradual return in the last following 5 years. New and modern bohemianism includes not just home decor and fashion but a whole lifestyle centered on personal growth, spiritual advancement, and the value of "self-care," especially for women. Consequently, hobbies, which are more gender-centric and related to the feminine tradition, which includes fiber arts, have also fancied their interest. Interestingly, modern Macramé is a global trend now.

Future of Macramé

Macramé is a technique of crafting that makes use of knots to create different textiles. As this art form has regained prominence in recent years, creative ways are being developed by craftsmen and artists to take macramé beyond the simple hangers of plants and wall hangings.

For thousands of years, that age-old practice has gone in and out of popularity. Nevertheless, because of their practicality, this approach will always be prevalent to some degree. Remarkably, products such as macramé table runners and key chains can be produced with only the hands and a few economical materials.

Chapter 2: Benefits of Learning Macramé

You do not need to look for a studio to teach you how to knit a knotty board, a drapery plant hanger, or a small key chain together. Boho and minimalist variations provide a wet yet trendy feel. Why did this maligned product of the 1970s find new life in the 21st century? You asked, we answered.

Knot, braid, and tie are the new things to unwind. Macramé has been out for a long time; now, it celebrates a fantastic comeback as an indoor trend. It developed from Germany via New York and London to Tokyo, and it can be found once again in the unique concept stores and famous restaurants. The macramé tsunami has swamped the beauty forums completely with directions for knotting. Therefore, DIY-lovers with smart fingers tie a knot above a knot in living rooms worldwide and turn every space into a glamorous gallery with macramé tapestries and plant hangers.

Old Design Formulas Also Have a Way to Unwind

Why do we like macramé, this traditional textile manufacturing hand-knotted art? The internet age has transformed our daily lives dramatically and led to, among other factors, a profound shift in customer behavior. There are indicators of a change in the digital environment to physical objects, which could be seen in architecture, construction, interiors and lifestyle, food, and fashion. Many people are already waiting to do it again. A new wave of do-it-yourself was formed, powered by the thousands of people in generation Y. We want natural products and unique objects. One consequence in the interior world is the excellent bounce-back of macramé, the craft of knitting from hand textiles. The beauty is that macramé takes a lot of energy, silence, and implementation, and it has something contemplative that generation Y is sorely missing.

A Group that Embraces Inner Peace

Generation Y takes a particular direction in finding harmony and inner peace. Like a counter-direction against immediacy, the motto is 'unwinding.' The fundamental prerequisite is the work-life balance. The significant return of this macramé is not so shocking from this viewpoint. Among others at the forefront of this trend is Sally England, an American artist for textile, who since 2010 has focused entirely on this old practice and rediscovered the elegance of knotting. With her macramé pieces of art in a large format in an extremely modern look, she has catapulted the conventional handicrafts into the present. Her works represent the need for individuality, natural resources, and the unendingness of our culture. She blends all exceptional technological know-how with Generation Y's fun spontaneity. This fresh, Bohemian-chic, hippy trend is spreading like a plague across the globe. Many other macramé skilled artists like Lise Silva, with her macramé necklaces, or the German visionary Dote Bundt with her workshops, are creating our vision for a different kind of biodiversity and patrimony.

The Macramé Founder—Sally England

Sally England is heading the latest "Hippy Age 2.0" with the macramé wave. She was born in Ann Arbor in 1979 and lived her youth surrounded by magical streams, woods, and plains. In this, she found a profound connection with nature. Maturing in a second-generation artist household, she discovered that her genuine passion for textiles and natural fabrics was awoken at a young age. She read a novel on macramé as a teenager, which was her mother's. She finished her bachelor's degree in Arts Communication first, then started researching old macramé published books as a side-job, driven by her respect for traditional handicraft processes. In doing so, she carried out significant research into the ancient knotting technique.

Sally England moved to Michigan after this and opened a workshop in an old Victorian flat. Far from a big city's quick tempo, she has chosen this as her platform to pay attention to the macramé meditative and time-intensive work processes. The unique tools are her hands. She does ordinary works, from thick ropes on the one hand to room dividers and large-scale sculptural tapestries on the other. This led to modern representations with remarkable tactility, including abstract patterns, narrow circles, and intricate structures.

The Knotting Art

The past of macramé began in the 13th century when intricate, hand-knotted decoration heads were made by Arab weavers, shield their horses from flying objects, and decorate their homes. The trade may, however, can be traced back to the Freemasons and Crusaders. The macramé painting traveled from Spain and Italy to all over the globe on 15th-century sailing ships. During the long voyages at sea, sailors knotted nets, hanging mats, and gifts for their beloved ones at the ports where they landed. Nevertheless, during the era of Victorians, macramé was undergoing its golden age. In the 1960s, as hippies adorned their skirts, plant hangers, and waistcoats with fringes, this ancient practice experienced a second revival, railing opposite the way the environment was changing knotting for harmony. Throughout the chic, innovative 1980s, marked by the Cold War, T-shirts made of knots and vibrant friendship bracelets sparked a swift return of conventional knotting techniques.

Physical, Social, and Economic Impact of Macramé

Do you realize hobbies can minimize stress by 34%? That's Good. Even getting out of the humdrum routine and doing something enjoyable will greatly benefit your well-being. Improve your psychological health and seek as a calming exercise to do Macramé. There's no question that this year is going to be a major year for macramé. To someone who wants to knit or crochet, this is the ideal hobby concept.

Essentially, it means making a variety of glamorous boho pieces using knotting techniques—such as wall decor, jewelry, plant hangers, handbags, and more. To get going, just invest in a braided cotton string loop.

Whether you choose to take up a relaxing game, macramé is a perfect way to unlock your ingenuity, stimulate your brain, and ease tension. Although it's relaxing and entertaining as a sport, macramé often has a particular function—the final product presents you with anything you can confidently show for art or sale or send to your friends and family as a thoughtful, personalized gift.

As a hobby, macramé will enable you to turn into a profitable enterprise.

However, its healing properties will have you hooked. Making everything with your hands is inspiring.

You may also use macramé as a regular relaxer. It's a method of meditation. You will start to experience and appreciate the flow and repetition of knotting a pattern as you become more immersed and involved in this beautiful work.

Also, macramé doesn't need a ton of equipment—all you need is wire, scissors, hands, and anything to hang on. Additionally, there are several resources and things that can support you and save time when you're doing your macramé dream.

It Serves as a Relaxation Therapy

Stress therapy has been a significant worry in the world today. With the rise in so many activities and busy schedules, there is a need to balance actions that calm the nerves and reduce tension. Depression and anxiety are other emotional problems that need serious attention. All these arise from the body's response to some events and casualties. Macramé art is an effective way of managing such stress. The processes involved in creating a piece of macramé art take your attention away from the stress and emotional imbalances your body faces and focus them on the art of crafting. The joy of having to create something beautiful is a good way of taking off unnecessary stressors.

As you craft different forms of macramé art, it helps you meditate; such activity brings about peace and calmness in your entire body. Therefore, many people who are macramé crafters are, most times, joyful and happy. As you create different materials, it indirectly affects the neurons that are secreted in your brain. Even when the emotions you're feeling at that point are depressing emotion, your brain can secret other hormones that trigger up happiness and joy within you. The more time you spend making macramé, the more you change your mood and state of mind for the better.

It Boosts Your Mental Capacity

For many people, macramé means different things. For some, the skill of creating something that appeals to the eyes is both mental and intellectual. Intellectual in the sense that the individual has to develop a really good design that makes his works stand out. This process indirectly increases your brain power and cognitive reasoning. You can use it as a medium to awaken your critical reasoning power, especially when you feel you are gradually losing control over it due to pressures from the office or family. Today so many have been celebrated on account of the beautiful pieces of art they have created. Sometimes you might not have all the necessary material to finish your design. Your ability to improvise and make use of what you have can boost your thinking capacity. Many of the early crafters of macramé, like the sailors, didn't always have all the desired components to build something nice. They only got the opportunity when they arrived in some cities and docked at some bays. This didn't stop them from creating better designs because they made use of the available materials.

It Strengthens Your Arms

Tying macramé knots and patterns helps strengthen your arms and muscles. For persons who have experienced conditions that weaken their arms and muscles, macramé knot tying can bring back their strength. As you continue tying and knotting, you will gently receive relief from your pain and muscle contractions. You will also discover your joints becoming free and loose.

It Makes You More Creative

Everyone is creative; all you need is to trust and believe in yourself to unlock that part of your brain. You are free to express yourself in what you make, and therefore this allows you to engage your creative side and make breathtaking macramé pieces.

It Helps You Grow

Once you are out of your comfort zone, growing each day, you become a better person. Learning macramé allows you to live an active, healthy, and connected life, as you spend time learning what other people are doing, get inspired by their crafts, find ways of improving or customizing them, and more.

It Gives You Time and Permission to Learn a New Skill

People are always looking to learn new beneficial skills. By learning macramé, you build a new skill that is fun and very beneficial to you.

It is always challenging to try something new because you're not used to the change. Therefore, to make it more interesting and fun, you need to try something that challenges you while being interesting.

Macramé offers just that—the perfect combination of challenges and fun as you slowly become better knot by knot. Once you create something nice, you'll feel quite happy and satisfied that you'll love engaging in macramé.

It Allows You to Make Amazing Works of Art

These amazing works of art can be used to decorate homes or even offices. They add a great touch to the vibe and general look of a place. You could even gift your loved ones and impress them with your skills and thoughtfulness.

It Is a Way to Make a Living Easily

If you've been looking for a way to make a living by doing your own business, then macramé is the way to go. People love beautiful things, irrespective of how the economy is performing! If you can perfect this skill, you could make it your little side hustle, which could easily pay some bills for you, and if you are serious about it and become a pro at macramé, you could even turn it into a full-time business, as you make breathtaking works of art that people will not say no to.

Chapter 3: Glossary and Terminology

Of course, you could also expect certain terms you would be dealing with while trying macramé out. By knowing these terms, it would be easier for you to make macramé projects. You won't have a hard time, and the crafting will be a breeze!

For this, you should keep the following in mind!

Alternating

This applies to patterns where more than 1 cord is being tied together. It involves switching and looping, just like the half-hitch.

Adjacent

These are knots or cords that rest on one another.

Alternating Square Knots (ASK)

You'll find this in most macramé patterns. As the name suggests, it's all about square knots that alternate on a fabric.

Bar

When a distinct area is raised in the pattern, it means that you have created a "bar." This could either be diagonal, horizontal, or vertical.

Band

A design that has been knotted to be flat or wide.

Button Knot

This is a knot that is firm and is round.

Bundle

These are cords that have been grouped as one. They could be held together by a knot.

Braided Cord

These are materials with individual fibers that are grouped as one. It is also stronger than most materials because all the fibers work together as one.

Braid

Sometimes called Plait, this describes 3 or more cords that have been woven under or over each other.

Body

This talks about the projects.

Bight

This is in the thread that has carefully been folded, so loops could also make their way out to the knots.

Crook

This is just the part of the loop that has been curved and is located near the crossing point.

Core

This term refers to a group of cords that are running along the center of a knot. They're also called "filling cords."

Cord

This could either be the material, or cord/thread that you are using, or the specific cords that have been designed to work together.

Combination Knot

These are 2 knots that have been designed to work as one.

Cloisonné

This is a bead with metal filaments used for decorative purposes.

Chinese Crown Knot

This is usually used for Asian-inspired jewelry or décor.

Charm

This is a small bead that dangles and is usually just 1- inch in size.

Doubled

These are patterns that have been repeated in a single pattern.

Double Half Hitch (DHH)

This is a specific type of knot that's not used in many crafts, except for really decorative, unusual ones. This is made by making sure that 2 half hitches are resting beside each other.

Diameter

This describes the material's width based on millimeters.

Diagonal

This is a row of knots or cords that runs from the upper left side to the opposite.

Excess Material

This describes the part of the thread that's left hanging after you have knotted the fabric. Sometimes, it's hidden using fringes, too.

Fusion Knots

This starts with a knot so you can make a new design.

Fringe

This technique allows cords to dangle down with individual fibers that unravel themselves along with the pattern.

Flax Linen

This is material coming from Linseed Oil that's best used for making jewelry and even macramé clothing—it has been used for over 5,000 years already.

Finishing Knot

This is a kind of knot that allows specific knots to be tied to the cords to not unravel.

Findings

These are closures for necklaces or other types of jewelry.

Gemstone Chips

This is the term given to semi-precious stones that are used to decorate or embellish your macramé projects. The best ones are usually quartz, jade, or turquoise.

Horizontal

This is a design of the cord that works from left to right.

Holding Cord

This is the cord to where the working cords are attached to.

Hitch

This is used to attach cords to cords, dowels, or rings.

Inverted

This means that you are working on something "upside-down".

Interlace

This is a pattern that could be woven or intertwined so different areas could be linked.

Micro-Macramé

This is the term given to macramé projects that are quite small.

Metallic

These are materials that resemble silver, brass, or gold.

Mount

Mount or mounting means attaching a cord to a frame, dowel, or ring and is usually done at the start of a project.

Netting

This knotting process describes knots formed between open rows of space and is usually used in wall hangings, curtains, and hammocks.

Natural

These are materials made from plants or plant-based materials. Examples include hemp, Jude, and flax.

Organize

This is another term given to cords that have been collected or grouped as one.

Picot

These are loops that go through the edge of what you have knotted.

Pendant

A décor that you could add to a necklace or choker and could easily fit through the loops.

Synthetic

This means that the material you are using is manufactured and not natural.

Symmetry

This means that the knots are balanced.

Standing End

This is the end of the cord you have secured so that the knot would be constructed appropriately.

Texture

This describes how the cord feels like in your hand.

Tension or Taut

This is the term given to holding cords that have been secured or pulled straight to be tighter than the other working cords.

Vertical

This describes knots that have been knotted upwards or vertically.

Working End

This is the part of the cord that is used to construct the knot.

Weave

This is letting the cords move as you allow them to pass over several segments in your pattern.

Chapter 4: Training Before Starting

Edge Measurement

The making of the macramé lace must be performed regarding the type of work you want to do. For example, you can apply lace to the inside of your tablecloths or towels. In this case, therefore, the first thing to do is to measure the edges, and the part affected by the edges themselves. These applications could be very difficult to work with, especially for those who are not familiar with the art of macramé. At the same time, the way to add them into the fabric is quite simple: no particular processing. In this regard, before starting the operation, it is important to get everything you need to avoid having to leave the job incomplete. In this case, to work the cords, it is advisable to choose them of thick cotton.

Pin the Wires

The type of macramé you are going to make is a simple knot. This system is ideal, especially for those who have never made macramé creations. Start by pinning the first wire into the holder with 2 pins, keeping it taut and horizontally. Fold the cord in half and thread the buttonhole created under the thread itself. Now take the points of the cord and thread them into the buttonhole. Then pull the 2 ends and put them inside the same. After pulling it tight, tighten the knot tightly, so it doesn't come loose.

Thread the Cords

Continue your macramé lace by repeating the same procedure. Then pin the wire back to the base below and start over with the same system. Once the first cord is finished, go on to make the second; then continue to perform all the others that will be needed. Once all the cords are finished, begin to weave them together, thus creating a unique fabric. In this way, you will get a whole macramé lace.

Apply the Lace

With this simple technique, you have made a macramé lace you can sew wherever you want. For example, if you want, you can apply it to your covers, tablecloths, or towels. This application can create a particular effect and above all a return to ancient things that unfortunately today are very difficult to find on the market, but which are still very fashionable. But besides this, you can make any garment unique, original, and personalized.

The macramé is one of the most popular in the world of embroidery techniques. It is often mistakenly assimilated to lace or a pleasant intertwining of knots, while instead, it is a type of knot lace with very ancient and deep roots. The name derives from the Arabic word "*migramah*" and means "fringe for garnish." This term probably became part of the Italian language thanks to sailors from overseas colonies who landed in Liguria. In fact, it is a typical technique of this region, initially used exclusively to decorate the fringes of the towels. In particular, in the following steps, we will deal with understanding how to work with macramé.

Necessary

- Yarn of desired material and thickness
- Pillow
- Pins as you needed
- Scissors

Use a Strong, Twisted Thread

First of all, it is necessary to state that any type of thread can be used, whether cotton, hemp, wool, jute, synthetic fiber, silk, or whatever you prefer. The important thing is that it is well twisted and strong. It begins by pinning the knot holder (a horizontal thread to accommodate the "knotting threads") on the pillow/pillow with 2 provisional knots made on the pins themselves. But do not think that this technique can be achieved with difficulty because, on the contrary, it will only take a bit of practice to master it with good ease.

Choose the Boot Node

From this brief description, it will be immediately evident that the concept of knot assumes considerable importance in the macramé technique. Not surprisingly, various types of knots can be made with macramé. The simple knot, as we shall see, represents the easiest and most initial type of knot. But then there is also the flat knot and all its variants, such as the double knot and the half knot. This technique can then be worked on by making the so-called Josephine knot. The cord knot and peanuts are also well known and used. To work with macramé, it is also very important to know the reasons that can be made with this technique: the best known are undoubtedly nexma, jasmine, and warda.

Start With the Simple Knot

As already mentioned, you must therefore know that there are several boot nodes. In this case, since this guide is aimed at novice people, we will describe the simplest one: first, you will need to have a wire of not excessive length. Fold it in half, making the 2 ends coincide. By doing so, on one side, a "loop" will have formed, which must be introduced under the knot holder. Finally, it will be necessary to pass the end inside the loop just created.

Tighten the Right Thread

At this point you can definitely move on to the actual processing of the simple knot, therefore, first of all it will be necessary to tighten the right thread and hold it down and then we will knot the left thread on the one under tension. What you will have to do is repeat these 2 steps until the job is done. Obviously, for a successful job, it is very important to practice constantly, until you have acquired the right familiarity with this ancient technique.

Making the Object

Besides the knot explained in this guide, it is good to know there are many others (cord, shuttle, exchanged, flat, etc.), and just as many can be invented! The advice is to always use recycled materials, as they will make the creations truly unique and therefore difficult to recreate. As we have already explained in the introduction, macramé was used only to decorate the fringes of towels in the past, but now it is used much more. Lately, in fact, many bijoux, worked using this technique, are depopulating: rings, bracelets, necklaces, earrings, various decorations. The imagination has no limits and certainly, just as they certainly do not have the possible weaves performed in macramé!

Chapter 5: Basic Knots with Illustrations

Lark's Head Knot

This is a boundless foundation knot for any venture and can be used as the foundation of the project. Use a lightweight cord for this; it can be purchased at craft stores or online wherever you get your macramé supplies.

Watch the photos very carefully as you move along with this project, and take your time to ensure you are with the correct string at the correct point of the project.

Use the base string as the core part of the knot, working around the end of the string with the cord. Make sure all is even as you loop the string around the base of the cord.

Create a slipknot around the base of the string and keep both ends even as you pull the cord through the center of the piece.

For the finished project, make sure that you have all your knots secure and firm throughout, and ensure it is all even. It is going to take practice before you can get it perfectly each time, but remember that practice makes perfect, and with time, you are going to get it without too much trouble.

Make sure all is even and secure and tie off. Snip off all the loose ends, and you are ready to go!

Reverse Lark's Head Knot

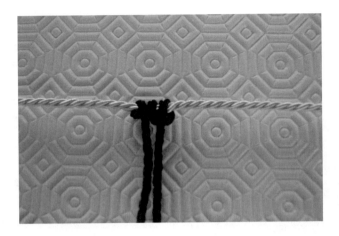

This is a great beginning knot and can be used as the foundation of the project. Use a lightweight cord for this; this again can be purchased at craft stores or online wherever you get your macramé supplies.

Do not rush and ensure you have even tensioned throughout. Practice makes perfect, but with the illustrations to help you, you will find it is not difficult to create.

Use 2 hands to make sure that you have everything even and tight as you work. You can use tweezers if it helps to make it tight against the base of the string.

UNDER

Use both hands to pull the string evenly down against the base string to create the knot.

Once more, keep the base even as you pull the center, creating the firm knot against your guide cord.

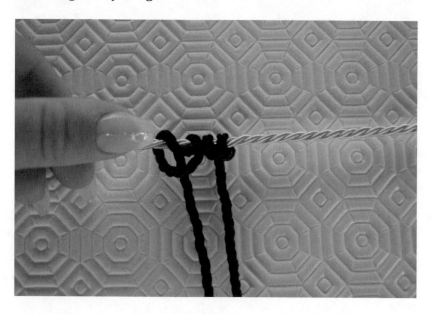

Capuchin Knot

This knot is for any design and can be used as the foundation of the project. Use a lightweight cord for this.

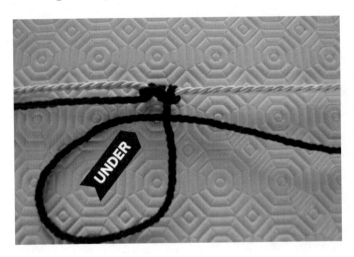

Watch the photos very carefully as you move along with this project, and take your time to ensure you are using the correct string at the right point of the project.

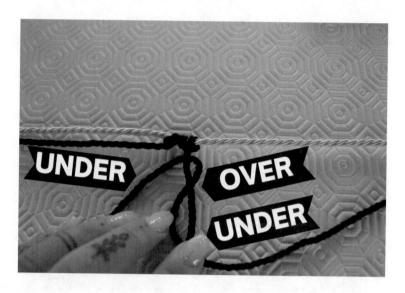

Start at the base cord, tying the knot in it, and work your way down the length of the project.

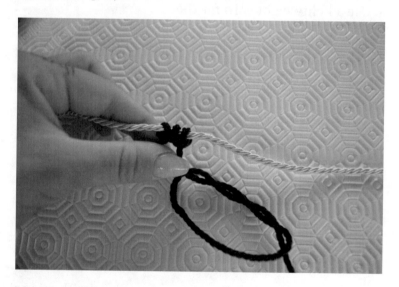

Twist the cord around itself 2 times, pulling the string through the center to form the knot.

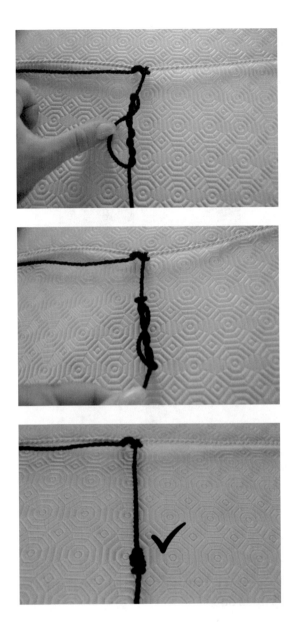

Make sure all is even and secure and tie off. Snip off all the loose ends, and you are ready to go!

Crown Knot

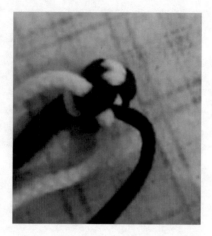

This is a great beginning knot and can be used as the foundation of the project. Use a lightweight cord for this.

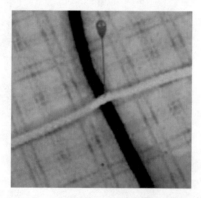

Never rush, then make sure you have even tension throughout. Practice makes perfect, but with the illustrations to help you, you will find it easy to create.

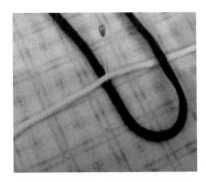

Use a pin to help keep everything in place as you are working.

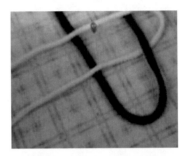

Weave the strings in and out of each other, as you can see in the photos. It helps to practice with different colors to help you see what is going on.

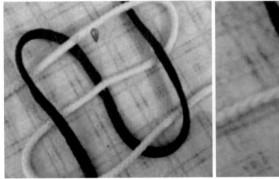

Pull the knot tight, then repeat for the next row on the outside.

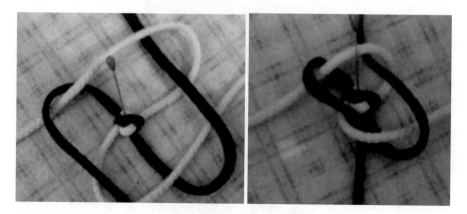

Stay to do this as often as you like to create the knot. You can make it as thick as you like, depending on the project. You can also create more than 1 length on the same cord.

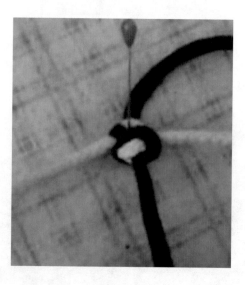

Diagonal Double Half-Knot

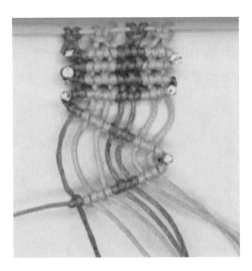

This is the seamless knot to use for decorations, basket hangings, or any projects that will require you to put weight on the project. Use a heavier weight cord for this, which you can find at craft stores or online.

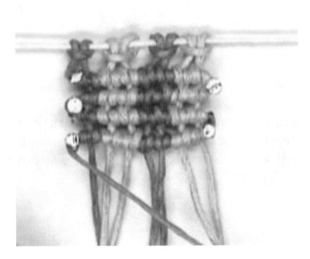

Do not rush, also make sure you have even tension throughout. Practice makes perfect, but with the illustrations to help you, you will find it easy to create.

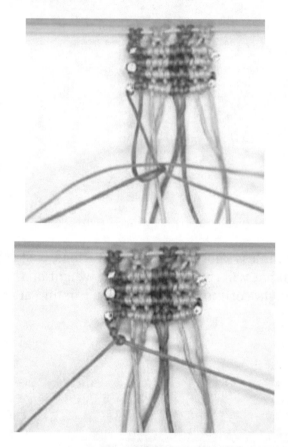

Twitch at the uppermost of the project, then work your way toward the bottom. Keep it even as you work your way throughout the piece. Tie the knots at 4-inch intervals, working your way down the entire thing.

Weave in and out throughout, watching the photo as you can see for the right placement of the knots. Again, it helps to practice with different colors to see what you need to do throughout the piece.

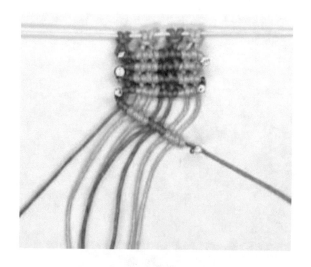

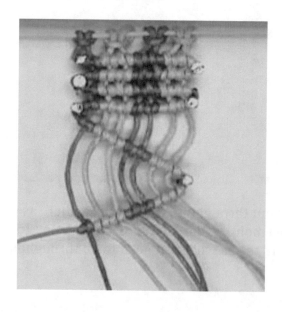

62

Frivolite Knot

This can be used as the foundation for the base of the project. Use a lightweight cord for this too. It can be bought at craft stores or online.

No need to rush, and make sure you have even tension throughout. With the illustrations to help you, you may find it is easy to create.

Use the base string as the guide to hold it in place, then tie the knot onto it. This is a very straightforward knot; look at the photo and follow the directions you see.

Pull the end of the cord up and through the center.

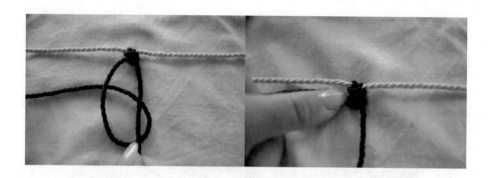

When done, make sure that you have all your knots secure and firm throughout, and ensure it is all even. Make sure all is even and secure and tie off. Snip off all the loose ends.

Horizontal Double Half-knot

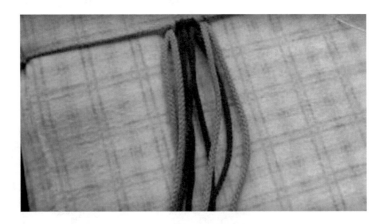

It can be used as the foundation for the base of the project. Use a lightweight cord for this by purchasing from wherever you get your macramé supplies.

Follow the photos very carefully and take your time to make sure you are using the correct string at each point of the project.

Make sure you have even tension throughout. Practice makes perfect, but with the illustrations to help you, you will find it easy to create.

Twitch at the uppermost of the project, then work your way toward the bottom. Keep it even as you work your way throughout the piece. Tie the knots at 4-inch intervals, working your way down the entire item.

Once finished, make sure that you have all your knots secure and firm throughout, and do your best to make sure it is all even. Make sure all is even and secure; tie and snip off all the loose ends.

Josephine Knot

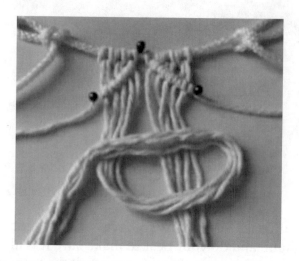

This is the ideal knot to use for decorations, basket hangings, or any projects that will require you to put weight on the project. Use a heavier weight cord for this, which you can find at craft stores or online.

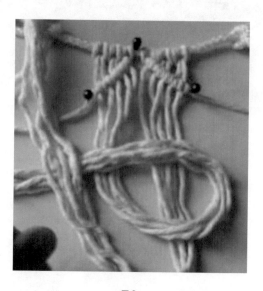

Follow the photos very carefully as you move along with this project. Take your time to move the cords correctly. Do not rush and make sure the cords have even tension throughout.

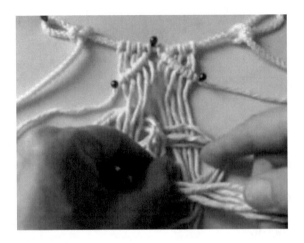

Use the pins along with the knots that you have tied, and work with larger areas simultaneously. This will help you keep the project in place as you continue working throughout the piece.

Pull the ends of the knots through the loops and form the ring at the center of the strings.

If you are done, make sure that your knots are secure and firm, making sure they are all even. It is going to take practice before you can get it perfectly.

Make sure all is even and secure and tie off. Snip off all the loose ends.

Chinese Crown Knot

This can be used as the foundation for the base of the project. Use a lightweight cord for this—it can be purchased at craft stores or online wherever you get your macramé supplies. Do not rush and make sure you have even tension throughout. Practice makes perfect, but with the illustrations to help you, you will find it easy to create. Use a pin to help keep everything in place while you are working. Weave the strings in and out of each other, as you can see in the photos. It helps to practice with different colors to help you see what is going on. Pull the knot tight, then repeat for the row on the outside.

Continue doing this as often as you like to create the knot. You can make it as thick as you like, depending on the project. You can also create more than 1 length on the same cord.

Half Knots and Square Knots

One of the most commonly used macramé knots is a square knot, and it can also be generated as a left or a right-facing knot. The half-knot is actually half a knot in a rectangle. This may be left or right facing; it entirely depends on which side you work from.

Square knots require at least 4 cords (2 active cords and 2 filler strings) but may provide more. The operating strings are the first and the last ones. We will name them as string 1 and string 4 in operation. The cables in the center are filler cables, so we're going to list those 2 and 3. Such cords swap locations but still maintain their initial numbering.

A square knot (left facing) on the left side of the completed knot has a vertical hump. Take your first cord (operational cord one) and pass it over the middle cords (filler cords 2 and 3) to the right and under your final cord (operational cord 4). Take operational cord 4 and shift it under all filler cords and over operational cord 1 to the left. Push all operating cords to close, leaving cords parallel to the filler. It is a half-square knot faced to the left. Functional cords currently swapped places on the right with functional cord 1 and operating cord 4 on the left. Taking running cord 1 and pass it over the 2 filler cords to the left and under operating cord four. Take functioning cord 4 and shift it under all filler strings and overworking cord 1 to the right. Pull and tie all active strings. Hold cables straight on the material. It completes the square knot to the left side.

A half-knot and square knot facing the right side of the completed knot has a vertical hump. Remove the last cord (cord four) and transfer it over the filler cords (strings 2 and 3) and under the first cord (cord one) to the left. Take working cord 1 and push it under the filler cords and overworking cord 4 to the center. Pull and lock all strings, making it clear. That is a half-square knot facing right. Functional cords now have positions swapped, and working cord 1 is on the right and working cord 4 on the left. Take work cord 4 over to the side, over the cords of the filler, and underworking cord one. Take job cord 1 and shift it to the left, beneath the filler cords and above working cord four. Pull and tie all active strings. It is a knot in a square facing right.

Chapter 6: Material, Equipment, and Tools

There are several recognized fabrics used to do macramé. These include silk, rayon, raffia threads, shoe sewing threads, cotton threads, jute, cloth strips, leather strips, shoelaces, and other lightweights, malleable, foldable, durable, and hand safe fabrics. Yet jute, silk, linen, and cotton are the most common fabrics used for macramé as they tie easily, come in several sizes, can be dyed, and are readily available. Any yarn comes with wax, creosote, or scale finish on it. Besides, any material is suitable for macramé, which can be bought in incredible lengths and seems to be pliable. Jute, raffia, cotton, and rayon threads are indigenous to the materials described above.

The possible origins of macramé were linen, hemp, jute, and other fabrics, which were mainly used for clothing and nets. As travelers and merchants collected various forms of material from the territories they traveled, they helped build the art and move it on. Fast forward to the modern-day, when we have emerging technology, fabrics, and most importantly, the Internet, you have the most incredible array of materials, beads, and findings to produce just about everything you can imagine.

Nevertheless, macramé requires more than just yarn, findings, and beads. You probably already have many of the materials you'll need to create the designs. You can easily purchase something you don't have onboard at your nearest art shop or, in certain situations, even your nearest hardware store.

Cords

If you can make a knot into it, you might use it to macramé. Waxed hemp and waxed linen are 2 of the most popular fibers used for working macramé. The wax covering on such strings helps them hold a tie extraordinarily well. Your ties and the following knot patterns will be very well defined. Art shops and beads sell those cords, or you can quickly find them in online stores.

Another common macramé fabric is rattail, a satin cord that comes in a colored spectrum and with at least 3 distinct sizes. In the late 70s, Rattail was common but never gone out of style with artisans who like to integrate Chinese knots or Celtic knots into their projects. It can be slick, but if not fixed properly, the knots tied in Rattail will loosen. But the results look so amazing that it is worth using this stuff.

Linen

Linen cording comes in a broad range of colors and sizes that make it highly desirable for many styles of braiding. Linen has the durability and range that most other cording materials don't have, making it ideal for macramé projects that need to be sturdy and robust. Linen cording is mostly used in wall hangings in macramé and looks fantastic when paired with other cording types, such as cotton and silk. The only thing to keep in mind while working with linen cording is that it will unravel quickly, so you need to be very sure to finish the project's ends cautiously.

Cotton

Cotton threads are weaker than jute, hemp, or linen and need more bending to allow them to hold together to form a chain. In most fabric and sewing shops where you work, you can purchase cotton cording or even from weaving suppliers. Single-ply cotton is used for macramé creations that you'll wear, like a shirt. Cotton cording comes in a wide range of sizes and is found in many designs of macramé.

Chinese Cord

This woven nylon cord preserves its circular form while it is running. The thinner cords, which are presently available in 0.4–3 mm., are usually more common with macramé. Look for the largest color options available online, although you may note the color choices for the thicker cords are not as comprehensive as those for the thinner cords.

Satin

This velvety string has a bright shine and is accessible in a range of sizes: the bug tail is 1 mm in diameter, the mousetail is 1.5 mm. in thickness, and the rattail is 2 mm., but in fact, it is now labeled as rattail. The string is relatively lightweight, and it does not help very much the form of the ties, which is not very hard-wearing.

Paracord

This curvy cord typically comes in 2 diameters: paracord 550 (4 mm.) has 7 strands down the middle, and paracord 450 (2 mm.) has 4 middle strings. Paracord is ideal for creating bracelets and some other items with individual knots and is famous for male jewelry because it is very thick. The cord is available in a wide variety of dark and bright solid colors and several multicolored designs.

Embroidery Threads

Stranded cotton and pearl cotton are the only two easily accessible fibers that can be used in macramé. Embroidery threads are fragile and do not keep a knot's form tightly, but when paired with tougher cords, they look fine. The variety of colors is much wider than with other strings, and thrilling color combinations are likely. Although embroidery threads are normally matte, a bit of shimmer can be applied for shiny embroidery threads.

Leather Thong

A circular leather thong, because it is a strong string, makes a nice distinct knot. It comes in a variety of diameters from around 0.5–6 mm. The thinner cords are ideal for tying knots, and the thicker cords are best fit for use as filler for winding the knots around. Leather thong comes in natural colors and a wide array of colors. Pearlescent finishes are especially appealing, typically in light pastels, as are the various thicknesses of the snakeskin resulting cords.

Wire

The wire is a challenging resource to use for macramé—but if you learn the craft, the results can be extremely special pieces of jewelry. The nature of metal is not to turn over and over again. This loses strength; repetitive bending allows the wire to become fragile. When you turn it back and forth, again and again, it will finally break. The thicker wire doesn't turn without a huge deal of energy. Many metals macramé is made from thinner diameter wire, which is simpler to manipulate. When it works, it will still tighten, so the less you fold it, the best.

Necessary Tools

Macramé Boards

Macramé projects have to be fastened to a surface as you work, usually using a T-pin or masking tape. In the nearest craft store, bead, or online stores, specifically made macramé frames are accessible and work for most designs. They are usually around 12 inches/18 inches (30 cm./46 cm.) and are built of fiberboard. Many macramé boards created have a graph on the surface and rulers along the edges. They can be replaced, but it's better to keep them in place using seals or shrink-wrapped because they can be handy directions when working on a project. Some other boards also include instructive diagrams of the basic knots in the macramé.

Tape and Pins

Pins are used to protect the macramé board project so that it wouldn't shift about while you are working. These also come in handy when you integrate different knot patterns and other design features into your designs to keep other strings in position.

The most common alternative for macramé is T-pins. They are good in scope, and their form makes it convenient to place and remove again and again. It is also possible to use ball-end pins used for embroidery, but they are not as durable as T-pins. Resist replacing push pins and thumbtacks, which are both too small.

Scissors

Most macramé creations are composed of thin fibers that are easy to cut with a simple pair of art scissors, like those you likely own. You need to get a set of little cleaning scissors made for stitching to cut the extra length when a task is done. They'll let you get close to whatever knot you want to cut.

Adhesives

Most macramé projects are finished by securing the final knot(s) with adhesives. The type of adhesive that will be used would depend on the materials involved. Hemp, waxed linen, silk, cotton, and other fabrics are perfect for white glue. Leather and suede are ideally suited for rubber cement or touch cement. E-6000 and epoxy are very strong adhesives used to glue together non-porous items, such as labradorite beads or wire, which are used with the strap of the heart belt. Any of these adhesives require adequate airflow while in use and should be enforced strictly by all health warnings. The most favored type is the third! A powerful and durable, non-toxic, water-based super glue. Remember the toxicity of the glue when choosing which glue is better to use for your project, mainly if it may come into contact with your skin.

Findings

These are all the small pieces, usually made of metal, used to create and complete jewelry items and other accessories. Some findings are used to conceal the things that are freshly made and some are used to protect the rough ends of strings; so, it is essential to select the proper shape and size. Keep a broad range of findings in your workbox so you can build and complete various items.

The Finishing Ends

We use these findings to finish the edges of knotted strings. There are increasing numbers of designs being produced year after year, and the majority are available in a variety of shiny textures. For better outcomes, fit the cord or braid to suit the inner measurements of the finishing ends. Some finished ends contain a clasp, but if not, you may add it yourself.

Cord Ends

This type is used to finish individual cords with lugs that you attach with clamps over the string; some are tubular and are therefore sealed with glue or by an internal crimping ring.

Spring Ends

It is one of the older finding types. It may be conical or cylindrical. Inside of the wire coil, wrap the string or braid, and use wire cutters to pinch just the end circle to seal it.

Cones End

Some cone-shaped or bell-shaped findings may either have a small hole at the top or end in a loop. Use jewelry glue to protect the braid in all designs for better results.

End Caps

End caps are rectangular, circular, or cylindrical styles of an end cone, with either a hole at the top edge or are ready-to-finish with a ring or circle. Use jewelry glue to protect the braid in all designs for better outcomes.

Trigger Clasp

This cheap spring-closure fastening is ideal for both necklaces and bracelets finishing. The lobster claw and a bolt ring are some of the available designs.

Multi-Strand Fasteners

Multi-strand fasteners come in a variety of types. The box kind is perfect for necklaces, and for macramé and other cuff-style bracelets, the slider fastening is best. Select the number of rings on either side to suit your project.

Plastic Fasteners

These plastic clasps are explicitly made for knotting techniques such as crochet or macramé, since they have a bar end to tie the cords. The fasteners are available in a variety of sizes and luminous colors.

Beads

Without beads, most macramé creations will not be complete. The accessible bead choices are stunning. The range of beads to deal with was small when the macramé started. Since exchange has spread across the globe and technological advances, the beads that jewelry designers have to pick from nowadays are almost limitless.

Chapter 7: Tips and Tricks

When creating macramé designs, your knots and finishes need to evoke an aesthetic appeal for your viewers. Though it also needs to handle the purpose for which it was designed, e.g., a macramé plant hanger must be well crafted to hold the plants in it without falling off. The same goes for other forms of hangers, chains, and various macramé designs.

As you deliberately pay attention to the tips that will be shown to you later, you will successfully overcome the creative blocks involved in macramé knots.

As a beginner with macramé designs, some essential tips would help you achieve better results.

Start with Basic Knots

At first, it may seem that different knots appear confusing and look difficult to handle. As you progress, you will get used to various patterns and knots, which would add beauty to your design. You should try as much as possible to get used to the square knot. It is among the basic knots you should be used to and a very good place to grow expertise as a beginner. It should be your most trusted and used knot, even as you try to incorporate others.

Attend Training and Seminars

As much as learning can be done individually, there are some areas of crafting that you can't be able to achieve unless showed by an expert or someone with solid knowledge. When you attend training, you get connected to others with similar minds and even others experiencing challenges like you do. This exposure has its way of spurring you up to better achievements. You can even make some friends and acquaintances who you'll run to for help when you encounter any difficulties while designing your macramé. At the training seminars, you'll be introduced to modern designs and easier ways of achieving better results.

Learn Online

As the world continues evolving, so does technology. This has fostered the introduction of tons of information on the Internet, which has become a global village where you can get various information on various subject matters. When you surf the internet, you come across relevant information about macramé and other available techniques. Learning has gone past physical meetings and coordinated trainings. You can hop on to virtual learning platforms with visual aids to make you understand what you are doing much better. You get to see the person twist his hands, perform the loop, and so on. You can even get books online embedded with step-by-step pictures on how you can perform a series of knots. As you follow them, you experience the ease with which these designs are created.

Be Expressive with Your Art

The mistake most people make is that they want to be so uptight with their designs so that they don't miss out on already set standards. The truth is that no matter how well you tend to imitate others and follow their guidance, you will always have your unique area of strength. Don't be afraid of making mistakes. A lot of mistakes are what have propelled so many of the world's greatest inventions. Your mistake might be a classic masterpiece for someone else. It all depends on how you view it. Allow your creativity to guide you into the best designs. Even though some people do it for the fun of creating macramé materials, others do it as a source of daily income. People will only pay you according to the beauty they see when they look at your design. Don't hold back yourself and don't be too hard on yourself, either.

Be Patient

Give yourself time to get used to the art, continue experimenting with the various patterns you have learned, and keep on developing your macramé knot skills. When learning, try infusing your ideas into the design; it makes you discover things faster. Patiently correct mistakes you notice, and don't give up on yourself. Sometimes, learning a particular knot or pattern may take you days and even sleepless nights; don't allow it to deter you from pushing on. Eventually, you'll get it if you don't give up. Most of the time, you'll find yourself correcting mistakes and revisiting old designs before proceeding to better ones.

Avoid Stress

You know many eager folks want to do so much within the limits of their knowledge and experience. This makes them avoid breaks and relaxation periods. They feel it affects their workflow. The truth is that there is a limit to which you can stretch your body system. You can't be tough on your muscles and avoid them from relaxing. Macramé crafting takes lots of energy and can be very draining at times.

Start Off with the Right Materials

You will find cotton more convenient and easier to use as a material for creating macramé. I'm not saying that others are not suitable for you. I'm advising that as a learner, you start with materials that are soft and easy to handle. You can use them in quite a variety of color combinations and styles. It is recommended over nylon for its homely and comfortable traits. Another good option to start from would be the regular use of chunky wool. You should realize that it is safer to start your cord size with a 3 mm. diameter so that the key strings would fit both plant hangers and small to medium wall hangings.

Try Out Easier Projects

Everyone loves to head straight on to something serious and tedious when they haven't been made familiar with simple tasks. Making things as simple as key chains and hangers might seem insignificant, but they are a great and gentle start for a beginner. As you accomplish more while trying to create beautiful designs of these, you can easily attempt more tasking projects. Even if you take quite a while trying to finish them, it becomes easier to attempt them the second time. Other projects like macramé feathers require lesser skill and knotting. The feathers, however, might require much patience trying to brush and trim the sides to perfection.

Stay Curious

For the success of any craft, the artist has to maintain a high level of curiosity. Curiosity is more or less an asset of gold while developing neat macramé designs. Your curiosity comes from your ability to keep getting inspired by the works of others. You can wrap yourself around other artists and works, even if they seem abstract to you. You will need all the motivation you can get by viewing and learning from their artwork. As you try to replicate the same designs, you will become the very best.

Staying curious and open to new ideas is paramount to creativity. Expanding your resources—whether it's through free platforms like Pinterest or Instagram—will ensure that you have a diverse range of sources to pull from when needed.

Use Good Quality Rope

Home and craft stores have a wide range of nylon, acrylic, twine, and cotton cords that incorporate a rope-like twist, ideal for macramé. If you are uncertain which rope to use, you can start by using a cotton rope with a diameter of not less than 3 mm. There are 2 kinds of cotton rope; twisted and braided. The braided rope made of cotton is 6 or more pieces, which are braided to create one rope. With the 3-piece rope (occasionally referred to as 3-ply), the pieces are twisted all-around one another.

Maintain Equal Tension All Through

This calls for practice. The invariability of the size of the knots is affected by the strength you use in tightening them. Continue practicing again and again until you achieve a rhythm and your knots appear consistent. You will need to find a balance between loose and knotting to avoid your design looking shoddy and instead have your knots looking nice and tight.

Begin Small and Simple

A nice first knot to learn is the easy square knot. This knot can be executed in 2 ways: the plain square knot and the alternating one. For many of the macramé designs available out there, the square knot is the core foundation. Also, this knot is a simple knot for a beginner to attempt.

Keep Your Tension Even

This one has to be practiced. The strength with which the knots are tightened affects the consistency of their size. Practice over and over until you find a rhythm and see your knots are consistent. You need to find a balance between knotting too loose and knotting too tight.

Get Involved and Have Fun

The easiest way to do something is to get proper help. The same holds for macramé-learning. Join a fellow member of the amateur macramé. You will find answers to your questions, be inspired, and share information. Expressing your imagination with macramé is one of the best parts of the voyage. Let your imagination go wild and construct something from the heart.

Save Your Left-Over Cord

You should make some attempts while you are training and try again. And having just the right length of cord can be your biggest obstacle. You don't want a little string, because it can be hard to add extra to your piece. We also recommend that you make at least 10% more than the mistakes that you think you should do, just to be safe.

Save Your Money

My advice is to always use a good quality rope to realize your projects. Obviously, a good-quality string will have a higher price. However, you don't have to be afraid; I made for you a list containing (in my opinion) the best websites to order your materials from. In them, you will find excellent value for money and many offers!

- Mary Maker Studio (AU)
- UnfetteredCo (via Etsy)
- Rope Source (UK)
- GANXXET (US)
- Bobbiny (PL)
- Hobby Lobby (US)
- Uline (US)
- Pepperell (US)
- Ket Mercantile (via Etsy)
- Rock Mountain Co.
- Niroma Studio (US)
- Modern Macramé
- Knot and Rope Supply (US)
- Knot Knitting
- Rope Galore (AU

Chapter 8: Make Money with Macramé

If you've been thinking about turning your love of macramé into a full-time or part-time business, there are a few points you need to consider.

Do a Thorough Research

First and foremost, you need to make sure there is a demand.

For this very reason, it is important to take part in craft shows.

Also, it's good to keep an eye on the craft market segments of websites like Etsy and Amazon. Find out if your items can be sold on these sites; if the answer is yes, there is market demand. At the same time, make sure there aren't too many competing sellers offering items that are too similar to yours.

Know Your Competitors

Before you start a macramé business, it is crucial that you understand what your competition is like. This means understanding how your competitors have positioned themselves in the market and trying to stand out from them. To do this, you could use different materials (e.g., sustainable fabrics), pay special attention to craft quality, and more.

Know Your Potential Customers

This will make it easier for you to showcase your items, formulate perfect descriptions that will appeal to potential customers, figure out which craft shows are worth attending, and more.

Create Your Website

I recommend you create your website. This will make your business look more professional, and it is also a way for potential clients to contact you. In addition, it is also a good idea to create your website pages on social media, such as Facebook, Twitter, and Instagram.

By doing so, you will increase the visibility of your website.

Take Good Photographs

Taking quality photos of your items is essential. My advice is to set aside a part of your budget and allocate it to purchasing a quality camera. Remember, however, to choose a background that is well lit. As an alternative, you can also contact a professional photographer.

Arrange for Shipping

If you also sell your products on the internet, you should also arrange for their shipping. It must be a quick shipment, and it is vital to choose a good packaging material to avoid damage to your items.

Pay special attention to this phase because many of the customer reviews are about this very aspect.

How Much to Price Your Items?

One of the most talked-about aspects of selling homemade crafts is how much to price your items. In fact, with a price that is too high, no one will ever buy your items, while with a price that is too low, you won't be able to sustain your business.

In this short guide, I will provide you with 3 strategies that you can use to price your items.

Strategy #1

There is a formula that is commonly used for this purpose that guarantees a profit margin of at least 50%.

Here it is:

Materials + time + overhead (for example: warehouse space) = minimum base price

This result must, later, be multiplied by 2.5 or 3. This is how you will get the retail price.

For example:

Retail material cost= $25

Time=10 hours

Hourly rate= $15/hours

Retail= ($25 + (10 x $15)) x 2,5 = $437,5

If you sell your products on the internet, you should pay attention to some additional costs. I'm talking about Etsy and PayPal fees. I recommend you to check on their sites how much their fees are. After that, add them to the minimum base price.

There are additional costs you need to consider even if you sell your products at craft fairs. I'm talking about state taxes and credit card fees.

Strategy #2

Keep an eye on the prices of similar items. You need to get an idea of the price range, and once you do, price your items right in the middle.

However, if your materials are of higher quality, you might as well set a higher price. If you have some very tough competitors, try it: set a slightly lower price than the average price to attract more people. At this point, as soon as you've built up a customer base, you can raise your prices.

Strategy #3

First of all, measure the width of the weave in inches, then you must multiply by a constant cost per inch. A good range is between $10–15 per inch.

For example:

Retail= 25 inches x $13/inch = $325

Wholesale

If you already plan to use large quantities of some materials, you might consider buying them in bulk. This will allow you to set a lower price for your items and still remain in profit.

96

Chapter 9: FAQs and Things to Remember

Macrame's retro craftsmanship project has many surprising components and stunning modifications. You should adopt the proper strategies and procedures to practice this art or hone your talents. For an outdoor and indoor product or item, there are several ways to start a project. Here are some excellent ideas that will help to make the best of your art.

Practice the Skill

Practice your abilities to prevent needless failures down the path before you begin to make anything. Remember, having the project going will cost you several bucks. It contains the costs you may need for equipment and accessories.

You can begin with a smaller practice project to improve your abilities for a bigger one instead of spending these efforts on failed attempts. It can familiarize you with many knots and designs.

Invest in the Fiber of High-Quality

The fiber choice is by far the most important phase in the process before beginning your project. Choose the proper fiber form that may contain cords, strings, yarn, or ropes. In this range, the fiber material means the most. Cotton, jute, hemp, nylon, etc., are the options used.

For beginner-level designs, experts often consider using cotton cords with just a diameter of 3 mm. To help the project, it is not only versatile and adjustable but also gentle and durable. There are also cotton ropes available in 2 varieties, viz—twisted and braided cords. For your project, select the thread that fits.

Maintain Sufficient Tension

You will become a specialist in the handling of a macramé project with the necessary experience. Here, the force used to strengthen the knots will mainly affect the final performance. It may even spoil the consistency of other elements.

For consistent knotting, it makes much more sense to perform the proper amount of stress you like. If the knots in areas seem shoddy, you can need to find the appropriate combination between tightening them and loosening them.

Select Easy Patterns

Start with a basic pattern to build your masterpiece, whether working on a starter or middle-level design. It may be a plain square knot or a square knot that alternates.

There are simple, easy ways to make patterns. In these models, you will learn to maintain uniformity. It would be best to use the independent boards or anchoring strategies to hold the work-in-progress stable in place.

Use the Right Amount of Rope

The number of ropes you require is 5–6 times the completed item's total length. Still hold the tip of an additional cord length at the bottom to create fringes and other decorative accents. You do not want a short rope, as it will thoroughly spoil your project.

Even attaching ropes later on is tough. Around the same moment, though, there's still no reason to waste the remaining strings. You may do smaller projects for the shorter cords, such as jewelry, bookmarks, or key chains.

FAQs

Can Macramé Be Washed?

YES. Macramé is very stable and does not readily fall apart. Even a tiny garment bag can be machine-washed at 86°F. Only hang to dry.

Can You Macramé with Jute?

YES. Macramé artists popularly used jute and hemp, but the lack of consumer demand led to nylon, satin rayon macramé cords, and other human-made fibers. Nylon cords or cotton are preferred for beginners because they are simple to unravel in the event of an error.

How to Choose What Sort of Macramé Cord to Use for Our Project?

When choosing your content, there are several points to consider. There's always something apparent to consider availability and cost. But with your idea, you will also want to understand the strength of the content. For example, if you want to hang a vine, you should use a stronger rope, such as those made of jute, ribbon, leather, nylon, or cotton.

Furthermore, you should consider a cord's stiffness. You should use shorter, more lightweight cords for jewelry, such as a cotton embroidery cord that is very smooth and flexible. When creating an outdoor project, you may want to use a sturdy and long-lasting polypropylene chain, either the outdoor plant keeper or an outdoor hammock.

What Cord Size Should We Use?

Depending on the project, you should select the thickness of 4.0 mm. or more for the larger decorations like the wall hangings or the plant holders. You can use a cord shorter than 2.0 mm. in diameter for the smaller micro- macramé designs, such as bracelets and necklaces.

How Much Cord Do We Need for Macramé?

The cords you will use for knotting would need to be between 5–6 times the length of the completed one. The cords that are your "core" cords used for the form but that are not necessarily knotted may just need to be around twice the final length. For having a fringe or the other decorative attachments at the ends, note to leave additional cord length. And rather than too little, it's better to have much rope. At the top, you can still trim lengthy bits.

How Do We Keep Our Knots Looking Uniform?

The easiest way to ensure that the knots are uniform, to make certain that the friction on your cords is kept equally and that every knot lines up straight, vertically, horizontally, and diagonally on both sides, you should check and knot, particularly when you are only learning. Confirm that its lines with the proceeding knot edges are strong and that the loops are even. The only way to make sure that the project is successful is to protect the project. You'll like to hang them from the clothes rack or a safe hook for larger ventures. Ideally, you can hang from 2 points on the project so that the project does not rock back and forth. You'd like to make a macramé board for smaller projects like jewelry.

What Is the Macramé Board?

The macramé board is a location where you protect your knitting project. This can be created from several materials, but you essentially want to make a firm surface where you can insert pins. A corkboard, a sheet of polyurethane, or the 2 pieces of the cardboard bound may be used. Without poking out the other side, the board should be around 12 inches square and thick to put a T-pin or the corsage pin in.

Why Is Macramé Getting Back?

Macramé was popular with the hippie movement back in the 1970s, but as a part of the latest tribal and the Boho (Bohemian) style trends in home decoration, it has moved back into fashion.

Chapter 10: Basic Projects

Macramé Journal Mark

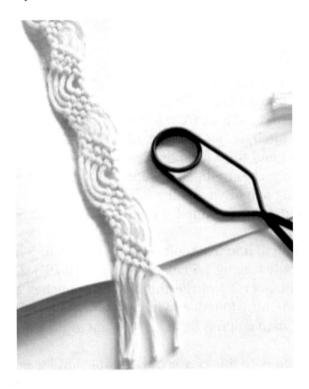

Never dismiss your number 1 peruses with this macramé screensaver! Why not get your hands occupied first, before your eyes do, to every one of those scholarly animals out there?

Materials

- Yarns: Phildar Phil string (100% grayish cotton) (cost relies upon the span of the journal marks)
- Clasp board
- Scissors
- Ruler
- Bunches used: Half hitch tie

Instructions

1. Cut 6 pieces of yarn multiple times the term of every journal mark. Leaving generally 5 cm. of string, attach the yarns to the clipboard to start hitching.
2. In the first column, from left, attach the initial 2 strings with a half hitch tie. Tie the second 50% of the hitch tie with the second and third strands. Keep on tying 3 all the more half hitch bunches to finish the line, continually using a line from the past half hitch and the following line.
3. Second, the third line from left, tie 5 half hitch ties for each column.
4. The fourth line from left to right, associate 5 half hitch ties generally leaving 1.5 cm. [0.6"], 2 cm. [0.79"], 2.5 cm. [0.98"] and 3 cm. [1.2"] of the third line of bunches above for the second, third, fourth and fifth half hitch ties separately.
5. Fifth, sixth column from left to right, tie 5 half hitch ties for each line.
6. Proceed with this crisscross example until wanted length.
7. Remove the 2 closures flawlessly and even to lengths of your inclination.

Do-It-Yourself Macramé Wristband

Experiencing childhood with the seashore in Southern California, the capacity to hitch a macramé armband was essentially the best activity. While those days are long behind us, we've never neglected a square bunch's essential procedure. However, this time, we're trading hemp and wooden dabs with additional up-to-date parts, for example, brilliant nylon string and gleaming metal charms. Great tying, fellow!

Materials

- 4 yards of 0.5 mm. Chinese tying line
- A connector or appeal or appeal
- A weaving needle
- Some scissors
- Level nose pincers (discretionary)
- A lighter (discretionary)

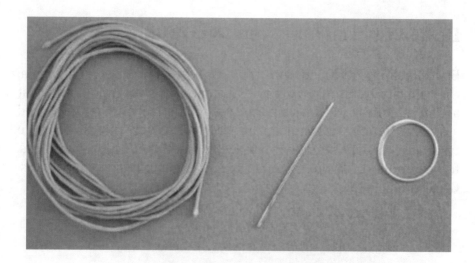

Instructions

1. Start by cutting the rope into 2 30 inches, 2 20 inch, and 1
    10-inch segments. Split the 20-inch area 50–50, draw the
    string through the pit, split it over the band, and bring the
    rest of the harmony through the circle. Rehash on the
    opposite side of the ring. These strands will be moored and
    will stay fixed.

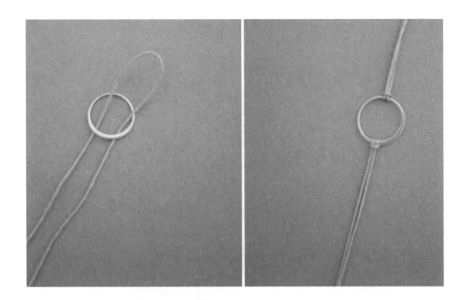

2. Focus the 30-inch string under the 2 center strands. Overlap the correct string over the center lashes and under the left line. Drag the left string under the privilege and focus lashes and into the circle on the top.

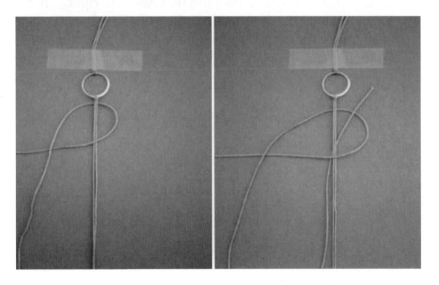

3. Push the tie solidly and slip it to the tip.

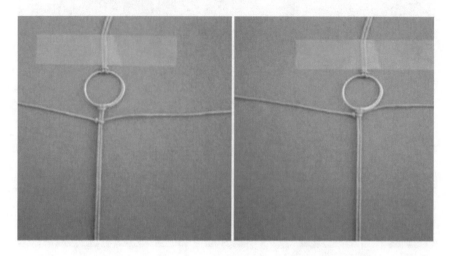

4. Finish the second 50% of the square bunch by collapsing the left line over the center strands and under the correct string. Drag the rope to one side under the left and focus supports and into the circle to the back.
5. Hold it intently and rehash the moves—left, right, left, right. Keep trying until the ideal length has been reached. Remember that the fasten will take about a large portion of an inch.

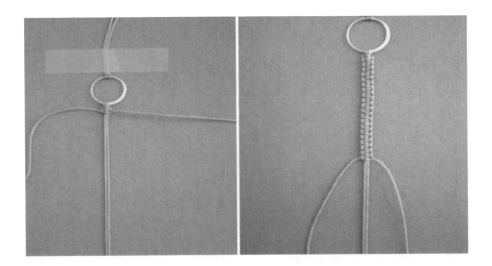

6. To complete the bunches, circle one of the ropes through the needle and fasten the center 3–4 bunches down the string's rear. Forceps will help you get the needle through the tight bunches.

7. Rehash a similar procedure onward the other line.

8. After sewing all tying strings, cut any abundance down. Save the pieces and burn the tips with a lighter so they can be fixed for additional keep. Rehash absolutely a similar proceed onward the second 50% of the wristband.

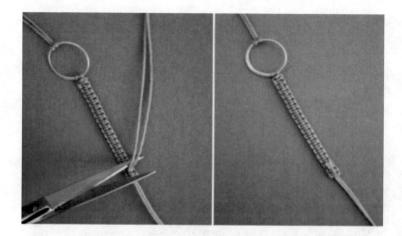

9. To make a slipping latch, transform the sleeve into a circle and cover the middle groups. Using scraps to tie the ties together on an impermanent premise at each point.

10. Take the 10-inch string and spot it under the strands. Begin tying square bunches the very same way that the wristband was executed.

11. Stop at about a large portion of an inch and sew the hitching strings to the rear of the lock. Eliminate your impermanent ties.

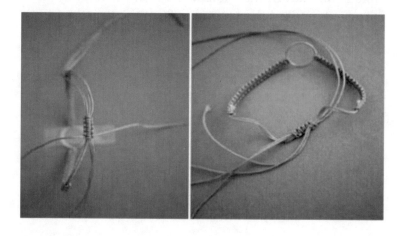

12. The 2 sets of center lashes are presently the adaptable ties of the sleeve. Change to coordinate the wrist and join the ties at one of the other hands. Cut any excess back.

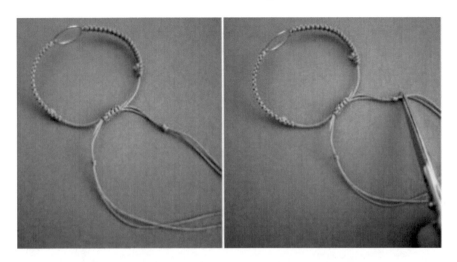

13. Your adjustable hitched wristbands have been finished!

Do-It-Yourself Colored Macramé Neckband

Materials

- A piece of cowhide ribbon (sufficiently long to tie and slide over your head)
- Cotton string
- Texture color

Instructions

1. Cut 8 pieces of 3 ft. long cotton string.
2. Crease each string down the middle and secure with a large head bind to the fabric.
3. I propose you tap the loosened cowhide immovably on the table, so your gems don't move about.
4. Essentially, the remainder of this example will utilize just square bunches. You should hang down 16 strings; consider them in 4 sets. Take the foremost gathering of 4 on the left side to construct a square bunch at that point, get string #1

over #2 and 3 and under #4 at that point, take #4 and circle it under #1 on the right side, start under #3 and 2 at that point come out finished #1 on the left hand. Presently fix this up to the top-holding firmly #2, and 3 will help. At that point, take # 1 (which is currently on the left side) and go over #3 and 2 and under #4 at that point, take #4 and circle it on the left side under #1, proceed under #3 and 2, and afterward come out finished # 1 on the right side. At that point, please close it to the pinnacle much the same as you did before. A bunch in line.

5. I used to substitute square bunches at the top. A square bunch for strings 1–4, 5–8, 9–12, 13–16 for the principal area, strings 3–6, and 11–14 for the subsequent column, strings 1–4, 5–8, 9–12, 13–16 for the third line, strings 3–6, 7–10, 11–14 for the fourth line, strings 5–8 and 9–12 for the fifth line and strings 7–10 for the sixth.

6. I, at that point, make a few irregular ties on the left hanging strings and managed the edges.

7. Tie the leather lace to match around your head, and, if you like, you can slip the ties a bit closer down the top.

8. I used Rit™ box coloring and followed the water and dye heating instructions for the stovetop. Then I dipped the necklace as high in the water as I wanted the dye to go down. I took it out a little, attached it to the pot's handle, and let it sit for a little while. I kept pulling it up a bit every 5–10 minute to get a slight look of shadow.

9. Rinse, and let dry.

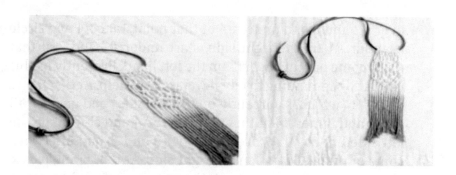

114

DIY Macramé Earrings

Materials

- Macramé yarn
- Sharp scissors
- Comb
- Small hoop earrings
- Clip or something else to clip the earring. I used a chopstick and clip, or you could use a clothing pin

Instructions

1. They're going for quite a bit of money, even though they're pretty easy to make. I tried to design them with a simple knot so they couldn't end up being too big.
2. I chose to use the fast and quick square knot and just wanted 3 square knots per earring for those macramé earrings.

3. You will see all of my scraps above, which I began by opening the threads. They disintegrate into 4 strands.

4. I laid them down, then put 2 of them on the earrings for the top loops. I opened them beforehand because I liked the look better and didn't want to take the whole strand to lither the earrings in weight.

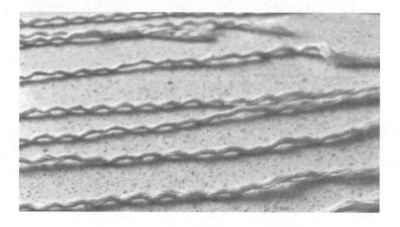

5. Loop them over the earring of the hoop, which is likewise the way you start any wall-hanging macramé.

6. You can see the 2 strands above and underneath. I'm showing you how the loop is shaped. It's quick.
7. For growing hoop, use 4 looped strands of 2 as can be seen below.

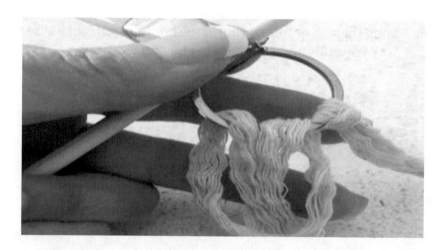

8. It's after that the square ties fall in.
9. The key to the square knot is alternating which string you are overlaying in the foreground. If you don't alternate, you will make a spiral knot that I love too, but didn't want.

10. Below is the exact configuration of the 3-square knots, which I attached to the hoops. I'm showing it to you in a loose

version to see how it is set up better. I pulled everything tightly for the macramé earrings, though.

11. In the end, you comb the open ends and give them a haircut to come up with your desired shape of the macramé earrings.

Plant Hanger Bella

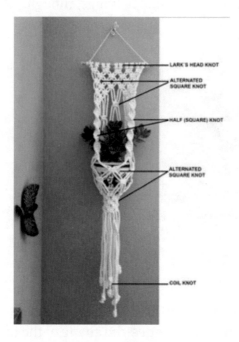

Plant hanger of 60 cm/23.6 in (not counting the fringe)

Materials

- 6 strands of a cord of 13 feet and 1,5 inches (4 meters)
- 4 strands of 16 feet and 4,8 inches (5 meters), and a wooden stick of 11,8 inches (30 cm.)
- Used knots: half knot, Lark's head knot, (Alternating) square knot, and coil knot.

Instructions

1. Fold all strands in half and tie them to the wooden stick with Lark's head knot. The longest strands are on the outer side (2 strands on the left side and 2 on the right).

2. Make 4 rows of alternating square knots. (See knot guide for explanation)

3. In the fifth row, you only make 2 alternating square knots on the right and 2 on the left.

4. In the sixth row, you only tie 1 alternating square on each side.

5. Then, with the 4 strands on the side, you tie 25 half (square) knots. Do this for both sides, the left and right sides.

6. Take 4 strands from the middle of the plant hanger, first drop down 2,4 inches (6 cm. of no knots) and tie a square knot with the 4 center strands. With the 4 strands next to the middle, drop down 3,15 inches (8 cm. of no knots), and tie a square knot. Do this for both sides (left and right).

7. Drop down 2,4 inches (6 cm. of no knots) and tie 2 (alternated) square knots by taking 2 strands from both sides (right and left group). Then 3 alternating square knots with the other groups. These knots must be about at the same height where the strands with the half knots have ended.

8. Take the 2 outer strands of the left group, which you made 25 half knots, and take the 2 outer strands of the group on the right. First, dropping down 2,4 inches (6 cm. of no knots), you tie a square knot with these 4 strands.

9. Do the same with the rest of the leftover strands, make groups of 4 strands, and tie alternated square knots on the same height as the one you made in step 8. Drop down 2,4 inches (6 cm. of no knots) and make another row of alternated square knots using all strands.

10. Drop down 2,4 inches (6 cm. of no knots) and make 5 rows of alternated square knots. Be careful: this time, leave NO space in between the alternated square knots, and you make them as tight as possible.

11. Drop down as many inches/cm. as you want to make the fringe and tie at all ends a coil knot.

12. Then cut off all strands directly under each coil knot.

Chapter 11: More Basic Macramé Projects

Knotless Macramé Plant Hanger

Do many knotting techniques scare you from making a macramé hanger? If your answer is yes, then this macramé plant hanger is ideal for you. There are no knots needed in this hanger. Yes, you read it right "No knots are involved." This hanger is super easy to make to add elegance and style to your space.

Materials

- Cotton rope
- Colored yarns
- A pair of sharp scissors
- Hook to hang the plant hanger
- Ruler or an inch tape
- Wooden or metal ring of 2 inches
- Few rubbers band
- Glue gun
- A toothpick or a needle

Instructions

1. Gather all the supplies mentioned above.
2. Cut the cotton rope into 4 pieces. Each piece should be 75 inches long.
3. Next, take the metal/wooden ring. Pass the ropes through it till the ends of ropes meet at the same level.

4. Now you will have 8 pieces of string. Gather them properly and tie a rubber band to hold them in place.
5. With the help of the measuring tape/ruler, measure down 4 inches and then tie another rubber band.

6. Repeat step 5. This time, place the measuring tape or ruler on the second rubber band and mark 3 inches. Tie the third rubber band.
7. The space between the rubber bands will help you wrap your yarn firmly around it.
8. Take the yarn to place it over the rope. With the help of a glue gun, adhere its one end to the rope.
9. Start wrapping the yarn from the first rubber band to the second.

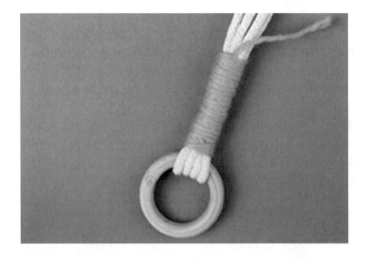

10. Once you are done wrapping the first yarn, tuck its end inside the wrapping with the help of a toothpick or a needle.
11. Use a hot glue gun to stick the end of the first yarn to the rope.
12. Take another yarn. It will be wrapped around the rope from the second rubber band to the third.
13. Repeat steps 8–11 for wrapping the second yarn.

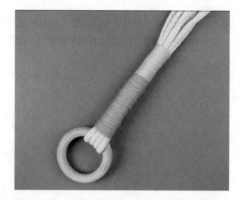

14. Keep the measuring tape/ruler on the ends of the rope and measure 8 inches above. Tie a rubber band on that mark.
15. From the first rubber band at the ends, measure 3 inches and tie another rubber band. This is the space to wrap your first yarn.
16. Mark 5 inches from the second rubber band at the end and tie it with a third rubber band. This is the space for wrapping the second yarn.
17. Repeat the steps of wrapping the yarn.

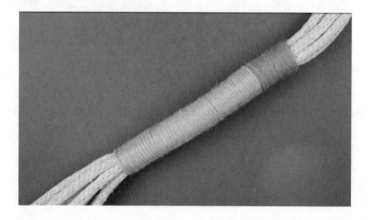

18. Place the pot or a vase in the hanger and hang it on a hook to add style flavors to your space.

132

Variations

- You can opt for more than 2 colors to wrap the rope.
- Use a multi-colored or a rainbow-colored thread to wrap the rope.
- Wrap the individual strands of rope to add more colors.
- Simultaneously, repeating the colors will create a horizontal pattern of the colors.

Basic Macramé Plant Hanger

This is the basic form of the macramé hanger. It uses only overhand knots, one of the basic knots we are very familiar with and used to. If you are a beginner and want to try your hands on making macramé hangers then, this plant hanger is ideal to start with. It uses the least of time and effort, yet gives your space a minimal and classy look.

Materials

- Cotton rope
- A pair of sharp scissors
- Hook to hang the plant hanger
- Ruler or an inch tape
- Wooden ring of 2 inches wide

Instructions

1. Gather all the supplies mentioned above.
2. Cut 3 pieces of rope of 50 inches each.

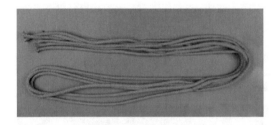

3. Fold all the 3 pieces in half; it will create a loop. Pass the loop in the wooden ring. Next, pass the ends of the rope through the loop and pull to create a lark's head knot.

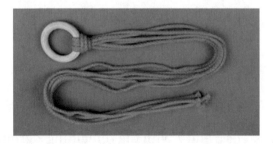

4. With the help of the measuring tape or a ruler, mark 7 inches below the top knot.

5.   Divide the rope into 3 groups of 2 strands. Take 2 strands and tie a half knot.

6.   Tie a second half knot in the reverse direction.

7.   Pull from both sides to secure the knot.

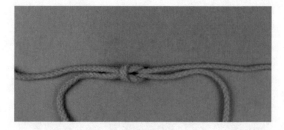

8.   Repeat steps 6 and 7 with the remaining 2 groups of the rope. You will have 3 knots in total.

9. From the first set of knots, measure down 3 inches and mark.
10. At this point, we will again make 3 groups of 2 strands of rope.
11. Pick up the right strand of rope from 1 group and tie a half knot with the left strand of the rope of the next group.
12. Repeat step 11 with the other 2 groups.

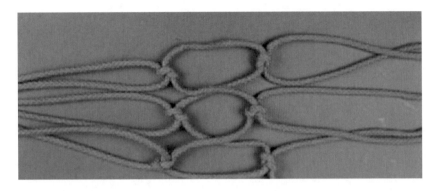

13. Mark 3 inches from the second set of the knots.
14. Gather all 6 strands of the rope and tie them into an overhand knot.

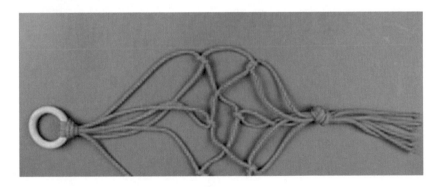

15. Place the pot inside the hanger.
16. Trim the rough ends of the rope to give it a neat look.

Variations

- Instead of using 1 colored rope, you can use 2 or 3 different colored ropes to create a hanger for a pop of color in your surroundings.

Upcycled T-Shirt Plant Hanger

We all have a favorite piece in our closet, which is very comforting and relaxing. We were never ready to let go of that piece. If you too have a t-shirt or a dress that doesn't fit anymore or is worn out, don't worry. You can use your t-shirt to hang your plant instead of throwing it away. This is a win-win solution for all the people who want to hang their plants and have a favorite piece in their wardrobe that they don't want to give away.

Materials

- An old t-shirt
- A pair of sharp scissors
- Measuring tape or a ruler

- Hook or a nail to hang
- Mason jar

Instructions

1. Grab your t-shirt and other mentioned supplies.
2. Lay the t-shirt on a flat surface.
3. Cut the sleeves and bottom hem of the t-shirt.

4. Next, cut the shoulders seams and 1 side of the t-shirt.

5. Cut 8 pieces of string. They should be approximately 1 inch each.

6. Take all the strings and stretch them as much as you can.

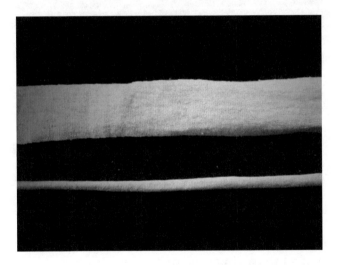

7. Take all the strings together and tie an overhand knot at the end of the strings.

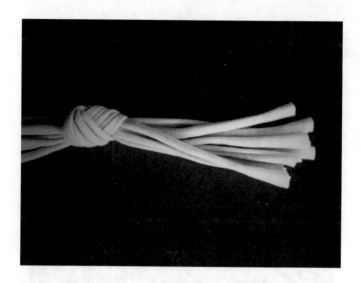

8. Make 4 groups of 2 strings each.

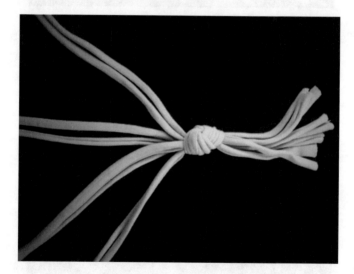

9. From the end knot, measure and mark inches above with the help of a measuring tape or a ruler.
10. Tie an overhand knot on the mark. There will be 4 knots in total.

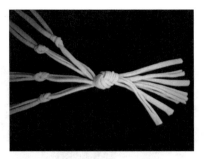

11. From the first set of knots, measure 2 inches above with the help of a measuring tape or a ruler.
12. Take the left strand of each group and tie it with the strand of the adjacent group.

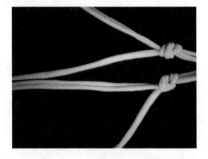

13. Repeat step 12 until another row of knots is formed.

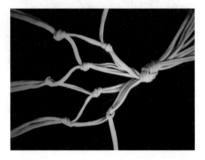

14. From the second row of the knots, mark 6 inches above on the strands.

15. Take 2 strands of the t-shirt and twist it till the marked position.

16. Repeat twisting the strands of the remaining 3 groups.

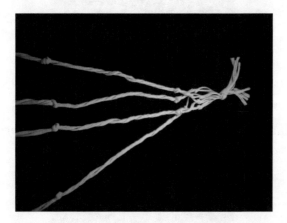

17. Tie an overhand knot, gathering all the 8 strands.
18. Next, take all the strands and braid them.

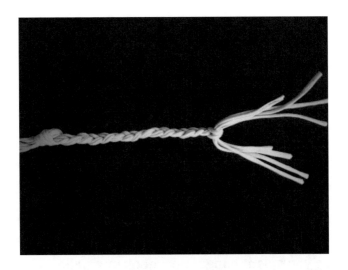

19. Take the remaining strands and divide them into 2 groups. Twist each group and tie a knot to make a loop.

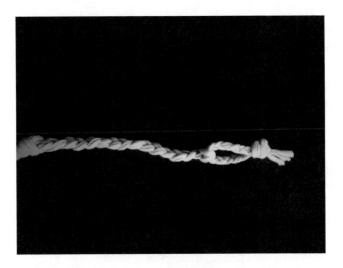

20. Place your mason jar or glass bottle inside the hanger.

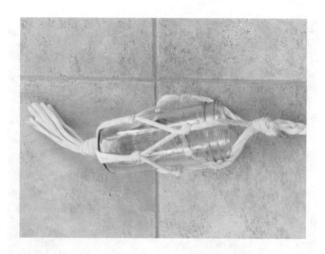

21. Hang your plant hanger on a hook or a nail.

Variations

- Use the strips of 2 different colored t-shirts to add more color.

- Instead of braiding, you can twist the strands till the end.
- Paint the Mason jar in contrast to the color of the t-shirt to make it more attractive.

Beads And Knots Hanger

This macramé hanger only includes 5 simple knots. Yes, that's it. 5 knots and beads to make a beautiful and catchy hanger for your plants. Macramé doesn't have to involve tiring and time-consuming knots in bringing life into your space. Sometimes even the simplest form of hangers (like this one) can look equally amazing.

147

Materials

- Cotton cord
- A pair of sharp scissors
- Measuring tape or a ruler
- Hook or a nail to hang
- 2-3 inches metal ring
- Wooden beads
- Drill machine (optional)

Instructions

1. Gather all the supplies needed for this hanger.
2. Check your wooden beads. If the holes of the beads are too small to pass through the cord, then drill them till they easily pass through the cord. But, make sure the holes you drill aren't very large, or else the beads won't stay in place.
3. Cut 6 cords of 50 inches each and 1 cord of 15 inches.
4. Leave about 5 inches from the end and tie an overhand knot.

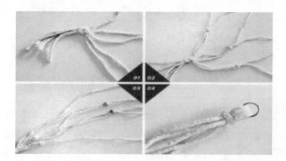

5. Divide the 6 cords into 3 pairs of 2 strands each.
6. With the help of a measuring tape or a ruler, measure down 8 inches. Tie an overhand knot on each pair.

7. After knotting the strands, we will again divide the 6 strands into new groups. Take the left-hand side strand and pair it up with the right-hand side strand of the adjacent group.

8. Taking the 2 strands together, pass the bead on it. Adjust its position according to your preference. I placed mine about 10 inches away from the knots.

9. Gather all the 6 cords and pass them through the metal ring for about 6 inches.

10. Take the small cord of 15 inches and wrap it around the cords to secure them tightly to the ring.

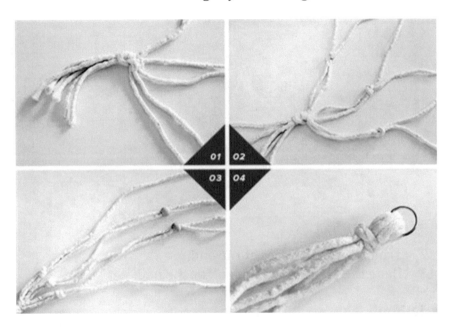

11. Place the plant inside the hanger.

12. Trim the rough edges at the end.
13. Hang the planter on the hook or the nail.

Variations

- If you don't want to drill the beads, then switch to the jute twine.
- Paint the wooden beads to add color to your plant hanger.
- In case you are not a fan of wooden beads, opt for pearls or crystal beads.

Chapter 12: More Macramé Projects

Fringe Pillow Cover

Materials

- 62 cords
- Measuring tape
- Macramé board
- Scissors

Note: The size of the macramé you're about to make should fit your pillow, so you have to measure the pillow to determine the size of the project you are about to make.

Instructions

1. Take out 60 cords and place them on your macramé board. Place these cords horizontally and make sure they are of equal lengths and in good positioning. Take out another cord and place it vertically on top of the cords you have on your board. Entwine the horizontally placed ones with the vertical one to make double half-hitch knots. Count out the first 12 cords from the rear towards the left-hand side, and divide the cords into 2, to get 6 cords on each side. Make a double half-hitch knot with the first cord from the left-hand side and then go with diagonal double half-hitch knots until you are done with the first half (6 cords).

2. Pick the sixth cord from the 2nd half, make a double half-hitch knot, and go with the diagonal double half-hitch knots until you are done with the 6 cords. Go back to the other half, pick the cord from the rear at the left-hand side, make a double half-hitch knot and make diagonal double half-hitch knots as you did with the other row. Do this same procedure with the cord from the rear at the right-hand side. Go back to the left, and do the same to have 3 diagonal double half-hitches knotted rows. Do the same on the other side (the right-hand side). Now, you have to entwine the 2 cords at the intersection using a square knotting method. Remember to have the knots and the patterns you make with them be of the same proportion, so the quality of your work will not reduce. Now, you have to pick the nearest 12 cords and repeat the pattern with them. Do this until you have made the pattern on the rest of your unpatterned cords. Go back to the first pattern you made, take out the cord from the left part of the intersection, make a double half-hitch knot there and start making diagonal double half-hitch knots, keeping in mind to distance the knots as supposed.

3. Do the same with the next cord just before the intersection and do the third with the same procedure. You have, again, 3 diagonal rows. Make 3 diagonal lines of the same knotting pattern with the rest of the other cords. At the intersection of every one pattern you just made, take a cord from each of the 2 sides, make a square knot with them, and continue with your diagonal double half-hitch knotting. Carry on with the pattern of 3 diagonal rows and a square knot until you get your desired size of the work. Now, get the remaining cord after you put the others into work, and place it horizontally on your board. Entwine every cord with the new one using a double half-hitch knotting method.

4. At this point, you have another set of cords and repeat the whole process you carried out on the work, to get 2 works of the same shape, size, and design. With the aid of a needle and thread of matching color as your pillow work, stitch the works with your pillow in-between the macramé works. This is when to give your project its finishing touches. With a pair of scissors, carefully cut out the excesses from the edges and make fringes from them. Check all the sides of the pillow to make sure you gave the work the best look it can ever have. Your home just got a new macramé fringe trim pillow!

Tie Backs

These directions are for a tie back measuring approximately 40 cm. (16 inches) long, but the length can be easily adjusted: they require 1.25 m. (50-inch) of elastic cord for every 10 cm. (4 inches) of finished braid. You may leave the braid plain or adorn it with beads. Given that the elastic cord is very rigid and hard to thread through when inserting the beads, it is simpler to use a tapestry needle to create a route for the finer needle.

Materials

- 5 m. (5 1/2 yd.) 3 mm. teal elastic cord
- Swarovski elements: XILION beads 5328, 4 mm. pacific opal and chrysolite opal, 54 each
- Seed beads 11 (2.2 mm.) blue marbled aqua and silver-lined crystal
- Nylon beading thread
- Size 10 beading needle
- Tapestry needle
- 2 end caps with 3x9 mm. internal dimension
- Epoxy resin adhesive

Instructions

1. Cut a 45 cm. (18-inch) length of the elastic cord and work the braid with a snake knot.
2. Tie a knot to a beading thread at the end of a nylon length (or equivalent color) and thread a 10-beading needle. Bend the braid from the end about 5 cm. (2-inch), so you can see the cord pattern between the loops on 1 side. Place the tapestry needle between the 2 straight braid lengths you can see.

3. Move the tapestry needle through the braid to escape between the loops on the other side. Leave the tapestry needle in place; this is the direction the finer needle threaded takes through the braid.
4. Hold the nylon thread between 2 lateral loops above the needle. Pick 1 aqua seed bead, 1 pacific opal XILION.
5. Place the beads through the braid at an angle, then take the beading needle back alongside the tapestry needle. Remove all needles simultaneously.
6. Pull the thread taut over the braid to protect the beads. Between the next loops, thread the tapestry needle again through the braid to attach another line of beads. This time the XILIONS order is inverted, adding 2 opal chrysolite and 1 opal pacific.
7. Repeat to add bead lines, stopping from the end of the braid about 5 cm. (2-inch) apart. Sew firmly at the end of the thread.
8. Cut the cord to the same length, leaving the tails approximately 2 cm. (3/4-inch) long. Mix a bit of epoxy resin adhesive and put a cocktail stick within one end cap. Place 2 of the cord ends in the end cap and force the remaining cord in place using a cocktail stick (or awl). At the other end, repeat to add an end cap and leave to dry.

Hanging Shelf

Materials

- Material for the shelf itself
- 18 big and strong cords
- A long pole that will be a bit longer than the wood for the shelf
- Rope
- Scissors

Instructions

1. Entwine 8 cords to 1 end of the pole.
2. Entwine 8 cords at the other end too.

3. Take the first 8 cords and make square knots with the cords.
4. Make the same knotting with the other 3 sets and have the square knotting to be of the length of your choice, depending on the strength of the cords and the weight of the items you intend to keep on the shelf.
5. When you have gotten the length of your choice, drill holes at the 4 edges of the wooden material.
6. Take the patterns you made through the holes and use the remaining cords to tie the closest 2 sets together.
7. Tie the other 2 sets.
8. Tie the rope to the 2 ends of the pole and hang it.
9. There goes a fantastic macramé hanging shelf!

Dreamcatcher (Tree of Life)

This fantastical macramé is excellent to give to somebody close to your heart and soul as a present.

Materials

- Single 4-inch ring of brass
- 6 m. of all strings, thickness 2 mm.
- 15 pony beads
- Feathers

Instructions

1. Bind one closure of the wire to the band of the brass.
2. Cycle the wire across the ring and firmly drag it after every circuit. To begin the following line of the network, precisely coil the string about the first string. Proceed to loop until the expansion is the required shape in the core.
3. You can append the beads elsewhere in the layout while attempting to make the hair clip. Shortly before inserting the bead, wrap the string and then move the string into the bead. The bead is then secured within the layout web.
4. Once the web is done, you can handle the ring with the string. Lock a ring edge with a dual knot. Roll the ring's size with the strap and then paste the ends to be secured.
5. Put a slice of wire, which is 6–8-inch in length. Append the beads anywhere; make sure you integrate a dual knot since the last bead. Move a plumb via the beads until it becomes snug. Connect the strap to the circle with a twin knot.
6. Choose an upper 6-inch string perched on top of the dream catcher to hold the final piece.

Conclusion

Macramé is the craft of making ornamental designs using knotting instead of knitting, weaving, or embroidering. The word macramé comes from 2 Arabic words, *"Macara,"* which means knots, and *"Mé,"* which means hand, so macramé translates as *"Hand Knot."*

To learn macramé, it is very important to stick to the basics. Keep practicing the basic knots. When you're ready, you can move on to the next step, trying more difficult knots. You learn the basics and then build from there. Macramé sometimes can be tough when you're just starting, but as soon as you get the hang of it, your knots become neater and your weavings more polished.

Macramé is a knotting technique for decorating or making a variety of useful objects, from woven wall hangings to furniture. It's a fairly basic crochet with pieces tied together by hand instead of crocheted into shape.

It's a great idea for children to learn macramé. They will have fun making a wall hanging in their room, or you can make a macramé a plant holder for them to use in their room or hang by the window.

Macramé is a craft that anyone can enjoy, even complete beginners. It is even a great craft for seniors, as it provides good exercise and challenges the mind.

With the step-by-step instructions, it is easy to be guided in doing macramé. I hope you have followed the instructions well and create a fine macramé product. A guide to macramé and some of its history, a list of supplies and basic instructions for beginners are included in this guide.

You'll surely have some fun with your children creating macramé. It's a bit like the old-fashioned craft of making friendship bracelets, but much cooler. There are plenty of traditional macramé patterns you can make, plus plenty of new patterns to explore, too. You'll soon be learning how to start your macramé supplies for beginners and how to finish it.

At the beginning of any project, creating an even tension that will prevent the work from becoming loose throughout the project is important. In macramé, tension is created by making knots using a length of thread or material. They are used to holding a piece of material onto another piece. The 3 basic knots you need to be aware of are the square knot, Lark knot, and the half-hitch knot.

Learning macramé can be a daunting task for beginners, but it doesn't have to be. By learning and sticking with the basics, you can expand your knowledge by experimenting and creating new patterns. You will be making decisions on what to do next! What knots to use? How tight should you pull the thread? Which way is the best, left or right or round and round? The answer is up to you.

In this book, I already have introduced you to different macramé knots and techniques that will come in handy with your projects or your macramé craft. And as a bonus, most of these techniques revolve around the modular principle of macramé, which will allow you more freedom to grow your macramé skills.

I hope you have learned something!

Made in the USA
Thornton, CO
12/11/24 22:24:14

563ecbc0-37a5-487c-a09d-a04a1add1999R01